When Pens Become Megaphones
By McKenzie Harpe

Contents

Speak with Yo' Mind
9	Directions
10	Silent Inquiry
11	Pierced Peace
12	Don't Forget Me
13	Discovery
14	Dirty White Shoes
15	Medicine
16	No Fun, Just Fear
17	Evicted
18	Woven Sorrows
19	Coping
20	Island
21	Trains
22	God's Plan
23	Faith
24	Self-care

Speak with Yo' Soul
27	Humble Beginnings
28	Avoidance
29	Odd Beaches
30	Rural Rumors
31	My Day Ones
32	Joy
34	Smell of You
35	Mama
36	Auntie
37	Sister
38	Red
40	Selfish
41	And the Beat Goes On

Speak with Yo' Fist
45   This One is For *Us*
46   Gimme That Back
47   Well Spoken, Still Rolling
49   Black Girl Magic
52   Rest in Paradise Aiyana & Breonna
53   Superwoman
56   Drained Dreams
57   Reconstructing Justice
58   Racial Battle Fatigue
59   Armed
61   To the Police Who Escorted….
62   Same Soil
63   Hands
64   Heroic: Ode to my Ancestors
65   Been 'Bout It
66   The Five Senses
70   Dear Hip Hop
71   Drowning
72   Reflections
73   Hey, Black Man

Speak with Yo' Heart
77   As It Was Written
79   Butterflies
80   Sappy Book Blues
81   Falling
82   Homes
83   Dramatic
84   Convenient
85   Learning Love
86   Fragile Love
87   Dry Hearts
88   Non-Essential
89   Ending This
90   Broken Records
91   Saving Grace
96   Abundant

to the peeps out there who find more ease in writing than speaking,
I hear you.

Speak with Yo' Mind

Directions

if you take a right
on Introvert Lane,
walk pass
an abandoned home
that says, 'Anxiety Lives Here.'

jump over
the mistakes in the road
and tread lightly
around that judgmental curve.

you'll notice a house in the corner.
walk onto its gravel driveway,
approach even though it seems
unapproachable.
knock anyways.

be aware of standing there
for a while.
the owner likes to make observations.

when the door opens,
you won't hear a thing.
it's okay,
just walk with them
into comfort
into safety
into peace
into joy
into love

...and then
you will hear their voice.

Silent Inquiry

adjacent minds
remain unknown.
thoughts held captive.

freedom won't be
granted
if lips are kept
sealed.

minds remain locked.
mine remains locked
until questions arise.

so, what brings you here?

Pierced Peace

I get annoyed
when people pop my peace.
they pierce through
my boundaries
like I left it unprotected,
ignoring my plastered panel
put up to keep out prowlers
who are too eager to kill
my pleasant solitude.
they repaint my canvas of comfort
into a picture of disruption.

is my profound silence that much
of a pest to their wildflower?

apparently, my peace needs
more powerful protection
because these days
the price is costly
for destroying my most
prized possession.

Don't Forget Me

so, I left my pen at home.

losing things has become
second nature to me,
becoming far too familiar.

items disappearing
in the blink of my eyes.

I
sometimes wonder
where do they go
when they never get found?
is there a gaping black hole
that swallows them whole
making them non-existent
when they used to be
here?

I
sometimes wonder
where do minds go
when they never get found?
is there a gaping black hole
that swallows them whole
making them non-existent
when they used to be
here?

Discovery

I lost myself
to find myself
losing emotions
I never wanted to find.

hope was lost
but now it's found.
does this mean I'm fine?

I lost the mask
and found the skin.
the soul was harder to find.

I lost the race
against myself.
the battle was never mine.

yes, I'm fine.

Dirty White Shoes

reminds me
that beauty
eventually fades away,
never lasting too long.

the outside
grows weaker,
appears less strong.

yet the core,
the inside
will always be intact.

does a tainted soul
equate to lost purity?
maybe it just takes
more work

to wipe it clean.

Medicine

it's free
with no prescriptions
no restrictions
or a physician's permission.

I only need ears to listen
to the sound of healing.
it allows my mind to transform
from a storm to serenity,
my remedy for happiness.

it gives me a chance
to find peace of mind
whenever I lose
a piece of mine.
my thoughts cleverly align
with the artists' words.

I heard
that loving something too much
leads to addictions,
but most days
music is my only redemption.
the only prevention
for lost hope.

at least with these songs,
I know I'll never die
of an overdose.

No Fun, Just Fear

some days my body
becomes a playground.

my heart plays hopscotch
while my lungs slither
through tube slides,

always getting stuck.

my palms participate
in water balloon fights,

forgetting to duck.

my mind plays
merry-go-round,

dizziness has struck.

my words get tied
in 'Red Light, Green Light.'

if only my lips remained tucked.

some days,
I can't help but long
for the sun to go down
and pray I find peace

when it comes back up.

Evicted

you resided in this home
too long,
rent free.
eating everything
devouring portions of joy,
drinking up all my pleasure
leaving me the tears
to swallow.

how shallow of you?

making messes
left for me to clean,
staining my carpet
with fear.
look at all the worries
you crumbled up
and left on my table.
didn't even have
the decency
to make up that bed
of lies.

see, I only came to organize
the thoughts on my hanger,
but now I'm cleaning out more
than my closet.
I'm kicking you out, anxiety

and I pray to God I don't
open my doors
the next time you knock.

Woven Sorrows

it's just something
about us women
and our sorrows
and our hair.

the way we snip away
like grief grows from scalps.
the way we straighten
like fear can be flattened out.
the way we cope with curls.
the way we twist and twirl
away our tears
as if it works,

cause it does.

I, too, have styled my sorrows,
choosing to coil my anxiety
into freedom.
I became calm with a simple
roll of my palm
knowing that finally,
I have my emotions
on loc.

Coping

I wish I could say
I run only
because I feel free
like gazelles in open fields,
or that I write only
because I feel peace
like pandas in bamboo shields,
and that I laugh only
because I feel happy
like monkeys with cheery appeals,

but I can't.

because I also fear
getting lost in the jungle
again.

Island

I just want to go
and be alone
where I can enjoy myself
in the present moment.

I'll wake up
with only the sounds
of crashing waves
and perfect breezes.

I'll wash away
my thoughts
like tides do names
written in the sand.

I'll write more permanently,
more freely
like there are no boundaries

because there isn't.

Trains

closed eyes
and slumbered thoughts
closed lips
and humbled hearts,
while waiting.

postponed hobbies
frustration
loud mouths
and anxious bodies,
while waiting.

weary feet
drunken dreams
waiting to be seen
to be heard,
while waiting.

time elapsed in moments.
giving us space
we never knew we wanted,
never knew we needed.

God's Plan

I imagine
if goals were people,
we would argue
all the time
about time.

yet
in the same breath
I would thank them
for running on His clock
instead of mine.

Faith

my eyes have grown
familiar with failure,
but like a river
nearing its edge
I'm still going.

watch
as my strength overflows
and my Godfidence grows.
this is what it feels like
to walk
with your eyes closed.

Self-Care

maybe face masks
never worked
because I failed
to take the first one
off,

but now I'm glowing
with a brand new
cleanser,
that's internal.

Speak with Yo' Soul

Humble Beginnings

my body has felt
the discomfort of chills
in the wintertime.
whistling winds against
my skin; the warmth
came from within
and around
as open hearts allowed
love to surround
the room.

my eyes have watched
miniature enemies steal meals
right in front of me.
yet starvation was foreign.
they were thieves in the night,
but never took a portion
of our love.

my ears have heard
the tumbling breeze
blow in to cool down
our car's hot degrees,

and we still loved with ease.

my soul has grown
to appreciate the love
because there's beauty
in the struggle and happiness
in what you have enough of.

Avoidance

in our darkest moments
we find ourselves laughing
brighter than God's rays in Georgia,
longer than any old-school preaching
on Sundays,
louder than clean up music
blasting from the kitchen,

and I cannot help but wonder
if laughter
is just another great medicine
with a horrible side effect.

Odd Beaches

I remember running barefoot,
allowing God's earth
to seep between my toes,

more grassy than grainy.

my legs made its way over
to concrete shores,
overlooking a sea of tall stalks
or low greens
or red dirt
depending on the season.

my hair styled by the breeze.
my skin massaged by the sun.
my eyes lit at the sight
of green boats afloat

far beyond my reach.

and I thought to myself,
this is such an odd beach.

Rural Rumors

I'm from down there where
every being knows
where we be.

someone's trouble and glory
from yesterday's story
will whisper through
God's breeze.
by morning light,
rustling rumors will roam
through the trees
floating to any ears,
doing as they please.

'round there,
small towns are filled with
heavy ears,
open thoughts,
and hearts bigger
than the countryside.

and that kinda love
is worth hearing about.

My Day Ones

a swift hello
after weeks
of our last goodbye

and that vibe still the same.

a witty joke
after months
of our last laugh

and that vibe still the same.

a necessary vent
after years
of personal growth

and that vibe still the same.

our secure connections
don't need daily connections

cause that vibe will always
be the same.

Joy

sometimes happiness
is energetic.
dancing beneath our
sun's rays
with the presence of
grill fragranced clouds
and laughter heavier
than smacked cards
on tables.

sometimes happiness
is delightful.
sweeter than
a plate of yams,
as refreshing as
an ice cooler,
with more soul
than old tunes.

sometimes happiness
is music.
allowing your body
to move
before your ears hear
the beat.
it's packed driveways.
it's joy with no concept
of time,
lasting past midnight
cause late starts
don't mean early ends.

sometimes happiness
is reassuring.
knowing where love lives
and that it's staying

with no intent to leave,
cause it's forever.

Smell of You

yesterday, I got a whiff of some Avon perfume.

the particles in the air
grew arms and reached
for a paintbrush nearby.

they tickled my nose
and entered the
tunnel of exploration.
brush strokes
lead up to my mind
and found comfort in
turning pink matter
into a masterpiece,
into a portrait
of a dark skinned, stern-faced
beauty.

a face with more glow
than wrinkles.
a smile that doesn't
represent present worry
with hands that made
the sweetest tea
and picked switches
from the nearest tree.

a portrait of a love
that's strong and permanent
even when your memory
isn't.

Mama

I'm sure you would
grow a forest
with one seed
and if somehow
shade gets scarce,
you would stand beneath
God's rays
just so your children
are covered.

I love you for that.
I am grateful,

but understand
there will be room
for you too
because that kinda love
don't fall too far
from the tree.

Auntie

I know a woman
who's not afraid of monsters.

you know,
the kind of creatures
that remove
life producing power.
the kind that makes a chest
one breast lighter.
the kind that takes away
kinky crowns.
the kind that invades the mind.
the kind
that's not so good
at washing away smiles
and laughter
and resilience
and strength.

cause I know a woman
who looked cancer in the eyes
and didn't even squint.

Sister

On November 20, 2002
someone somewhere
was wearing too much denim
with Ashanti or Ludacris
on high volume
like the songs were their everything,
their breath of fresh air,
or a God-given gift
wrapped in melodic fabric.

I got one too,
swaddled with pink comfort instead.

high-pitch tunes
filled the room
from a body whose
presence would eventually
make my heart smile
and skip,
my eyes dance
and roll,
my laughter grow
and disappear,

my nerves work
from sunup to sundown
with no pay
just love.

and that's okay
because
our bond will always
be thicker than any jean outfit.

Red

I think of tomato sauce
and how auntie can fit
warm gospel in a bowl.
its aroma flows
through the kitchen,
grows like them roses
Tupac mentioned.

I think of fingers and crumbs
at the lunch table outside
sharing love on napkins,
2 maybe 3 loves on napkins,
and being grateful anyway
cause the love isn't lacking.

I think of thirty-six women
in all their crowns and glory.
the way trap music and love
are authors of the best stories.

I think of lipstick, not mine
but the kind worn by
them older women
on the front pews
with the suit to match
and the shoes
and the hat
and the purse
JESUS!
if only I could age that fly.

I think of birds
those cardinals,
how they signify
compassion
love

loved ones
hope
new beginnings

in the beginning,
I actually thought about
pain and blood stains,
suffering and heartaches
but I wrote this
so, you can see
that most days,
happiness is a choice.

Selfish

I will never hold a grudge.
I'm just filled
with disappointments
because you missed out on times
we could've shared
beautiful moments.

in another lifetime,
we were two peas in a pod.
we'd laugh at all the jokes
my mother finds odd.

I'm not asking for completion,
just major contributions
like making sure I'm fine
amid all your ruins.

I dream of what it's like
to vibe with your persona.
I wish I would have known you
as more than a sperm donor.

I'm not here to blame you
cause I'm sure your pain
is deeper than I can see,
but I will blame the bottles
for making you love them
more than you love me.

And the Beat Goes On

at the age of three,
I became a dancer.
I learned how to make
rubber bands out of my bones
bending backwards before
walls plastered with glass.
I spun fast pass
a mass of girls
whose reflections were different
than mine,
whose presence was
welcomed.

before the age of ten,
I witnessed the impact
of my skin when
my classmate did not
want to dance next to me
at the barre; apparently
because she couldn't be
around Black people.
we were kids
but I guess not equal.

at the age of twelve
I quit.
yet the dancer in me
stayed.
I somehow still
tiptoed in white rooms,
controlling my arms
to the sound of their music
instead of mine.

stretching myself thin
failing to acknowledge

my identity within.
wanting comfort for them,
but not myself.

until that music
stopped playing,
and I no longer created
comfortable choreography.
I just danced in a way
that was done effortlessly
naturally
authentically
unapologetically
to my own beat.

Speak with Yo' Fist

This One is for *Us*

if I told you I was a poet,
what would run through your mind?
a woman who's creative enough
to make her expressions rhyme?
the one who sips coffee and makes
berets a part of her aesthetic style?
a flower-loving
soft-armed
dream-defining
writer.

nah.

I'm the voice for the voiceless.
expressing my creations
through aspects of injustice.
I let these words light the fire
treat my pen like some torches,
throwing flames and spitting truth
you can't extinguish this moment.

just own it
or flaunt it.

don't misconstrue this writing tool.
it does more than spill ink,
it empowers the youth.
awakens the slumbered
with a lyrical boom,
cause this pen is my megaphone.

it's yours, too.

and I'm gone make sure I use it
even if my ears
are the only ones in the room.

Gimme That Back

I took the pencil
from the man
cause he led me
to believe
what he wrote
not what he
erased.

Well Spoken, Still Rolling

I am
allowing my words
dipped in African soil
and molded in red clay
to roll down the hills
of my tongue, carelessly

cause they deserve fun
too.
they needa know freedom
more than me.
they needa be the bird
in open skies
knowing that liberty
don't end and never needs
a disguise.

you heard them language lies?

talking bout if I say "finna"
my tongue needa be fixed
and I somehow speak
with improper lips
if I say "before"
with the 're' dismissed.
as if my dialect and intelligence
cannot coexist,
that's a myth

rumor has it,
my words become invalid
once that Southern twang is added.
I'm only nurturing the flower
of a written seed once planted

by Miss Zora and Miss Nikki 'nem

y'all must don't know
these words be a hymn?
rolling to the same rhythm
of my ancestors' drum
and the same sound
of my ancestors' hum
might roll quicker than the feet
of my ancestors' run
for a land of freedom
that was stolen,

and just like the hills
these words gone keep on rolling.

Black Girl Magic

in a room filled
with sculpted bodies
lighter shades
and twitter hashtags,
there
in the corner
stands a broken mirror.
in front of shattered glass
is a girl struggling to see
the clearer picture.

she
is
Black
girl.

Black girl frowns
at her own skin
as if her melanin detail
is written in braille,
she can't see the beauty within
blinded by society's perceptions
her melanin 'too dark' to be
socially accepted.

so, by choosing to neglect it
is the way she corrects it.

Black girl flies
Black girl tries to free herself
of a cage filled with stereotyped lies.
she been told to stay silent,
speaking her opinion is too bold

so, Black girl stays quiet.

until the day Black girl realizes
that her imperfections are
her true perfections.

cause Black girl glows
Black girl flows
Black girl knows
Black girl rhymes
Black girl shines
like moonlight in the darkness
as her skin melts of honey and chocolate
with melanin dripping like water
from a leaking faucet.

Black girl.

she embraces
her hair of constant changes
from braids
to locs
to afro stages,
Black girl no longer thinks
she has to tame it.

Black girl.

she a magician,
watch as she sprinkles her golden spell
onto every test they said
she would never excel.
Black girl uses her wand
to rebel
as she abracadabra
her negative into a positive
her ordinary into phenomenal
her scarce into abundant
her "You'll never accomplish"
into "I've already done it".

Black girl leaves others
with looks of astonishment.

they gasp!
faced plastered
with an amazed gaze
watching her make a way
out of the maze,
no longer constrained
to the stereotypes they
gave her.

Black girl.

she on fire
with scorching brown eyes
and fiery thighs,
they say Black girl need to apologize.

for what?
being resilient and fierce?
for saying the truth
they never want to hear?
for being too determined
and driven with passion?
nah, there's no need to be sorry for that
BLACK GIRL MAGIC!

Rest in Paradise Aiyana and Breonna

sometimes
our bodies want to know
what rest feels like.

one where our bed
does not resemble concrete grounds,
and our blankets are not blue threats
to a skin so brown.
even during times
where comfort is found
because our homes grant us safety
to lie around

sometimes,
our bodies want to know
they can live through the night.

Superwomen

"The most disrespected person in America is the Black woman.
The most unprotected person in America is the Black woman.
The most neglected person in America is the Black woman."

a famous quote by the late Malcom X,

words that hold truth in every context
and I bet
to this day, we still feel the same
cause for years Black women
have endured so much pain
experienced so much shame
and despite our every obstacle
we still remain sane
being strong enough to save everyone
while receiving little to no gain,

but who gone save Black women?

funny how we be
the hero and the villain.
fighting for what's right
in the face of opposition
with fear of being shot
by coward-driven ammunition,
while striving to raise kids
in such dangerous conditions.
yet still finding time to uplift
our men and women.
that is the power
of Black superwomen.

we have skills that fulfill
spaces other than the kitchen,
cause the "S" on chests
does not stand for submission.

that letter symbolizes strength
of every generation
cause the works of Black women
produce beautiful creations.

we are and we've been the inspiration.

I oftentimes allow my mind
to start racing,
reflecting on a history
filled with our women's representation.

we are and we've been the true foundation.

with the blood of Nefertiti
flowing through our royal veins
and the courage of Harriet
freeing us from shackled chains
while melodies of Billie
sing songs of fruit so strange.
oh, how a sweet voice
provoked so much change.

we learned from Assata
how to be Black and unafraid,
learned from Angela
how to be Black and unafraid,
Black and unashamed,
Black with no intentions
of trying to explain
our worth.

I mean the value of Black women
been known since birth.
our presence alone
makes crowds disperse,
and we speak of voices so diverse
yet the same,

our echoes are powerful enough
to break chains
in a society that determined
to keep us constrained
so that we won't reach our limits.
seems like everyone is a critic
but we're forever being mimicked.

I mean I'm not surprised
people try to get a portion
of this power we exhibit.
cause we save lives
with this heroic trait
we've been given.
I know it's no secret

that we are and we've been Black superwomen

Drained Dreams

I know a school of fish
who spend eight hours
and five days
in dictating tanks
without necessary nutrients
without genuine guidance,
but still expected to swim
with broken fins stemmed
from broken bones stemmed
from broken homes
with no treatment to show for.
just expulsion and exclusion
with no adequate exposure.

how does one drown
in their own habitat?

sinking into stunted success
growing dreary of drained dreams
wanting more than anything
to be heard
to be seen
to be liked,
not cuffed or flushed
down a prepared pipe
leading to sewer waters
altered life
and pure neglect.

cause I know some kids
who just want to swim like the rest.

Reconstructing Justice

I cannot fix my mouth
to pass judgement
on those using any tool
to fix what is broken.

it might be tape
subtly piecing together
interrupted peace.

it might be a hammer
loud, with force
using great strength
to break down
what serves no purpose

and create what is needed.

in end, we are all building
shaping
forming
the house we deserve
to live in.

Racial Battle Fatigue

your breathing may
grow weak
speaking for those whose
breath was lost,
but it is better to fight
tired
than not to fight at all.

Armed

maybe I am dangerous.
this arm carries around
a notebook without a license
like this is legal,
like this ain't lethal.
to tell the truth
I load my pen with thoughts
then aim with precision,
spit fire on these pages
and hope you see my vision
this is more than just a poem.

this that weapon
I never reached for.
a heat released piece
for the silenced voices
I speak for,
bullets left untraceable.
I became capable
on how to make ghosts
out of my words,
murdered metaphors
seeking revenge and making returns
our voices don't die.

they just rise like roses do
from concrete
like balloons released at vigils
for cop stolen heartbeats.
rise like prayers
like truth
like lies
rise
like we're all past our boiling points
cause we are,
we been heated.

growing tired and angry
of a history repeated.

repeat it
like your favorite rap song
you know will never get deleted
cause it speaks to you.
somehow turns madness into melodies
and riots into remedies,
racial climates won't define us
cause resilience been our specialty

and ain't that what they're afraid of?

how we possess
bullet proof protective shields
over our minds
even when the rest of our body sometimes
isn't covered.
how we inhabit a society
that wreaks havoc but haven't
broken us yet
despite neglect
despite suffer,
we possess a fire
that can no longer be smothered
and
ain't that …. dangerous?

To the Police Who Escorted Dylan Roof to Burger King

tell me,
where was your fear?
a mass shooter
taken under arrest
handled with care and caution
not with gunshots and bullets
that could lead him to a coffin.
I guess that's the procedure
when the bloodline is more common,
even though it's a gunman
who left innocent people deceased.

I'm sure that's far less threatening
than a Black man who reached.

Same Soil

his hands grew tired.
knuckles on fire
skin scorching
from a bigger star
unlike the one
that gave him direction,
gave him hope
that was lost
when his identity was tossed.

his lost soul
left a void to fill,
and being a man
in foreign land
gave him emotions
he avoided to fill.
so, he kept them inside
and dreamed of ways
he could've avoided the field,

where his blood stained the soil.

the same soil
that was taught as his reflection
because of his complexion.
the same soil
that served as a connection
between him and this generation
of sons
becoming art on a t-shirt
made from the same ginned sin
that once had his hands hurt.
the same soil, the same dirt
that'll give birth
to the rest of the family tree.

Hands

his hands made love
with his pockets
because the winter stole
his warmth.

his hands made love
with the trigger
because bigotry stole
his senses.

her hands made love
with the casket
because Amerikkka stole
her son.

Heroic: Ode to My Ancestors

I've seen courage
take the backseat
of driven fear.

I've watched tongues
remain still
in the midst
of spoken hate.

I've noticed eyes
ram shut
in the sight of injustice,

but I know heroes who
fought with broken bones.

Been 'Bout It

I be shaking my crossed leg
in cushioned seats

clenching my fixed jaws
extra tight with tension

tapping my anxious fingers
on flat surfaces

wood
wishing a racist would

go ahead
spew out your ignorance

show me who raised you
and I'll gladly return the favor.

The Five Senses

Number One: Touch

how does it feel
to place your hands
on something that's
not yours?
like land
like gold
like Black bodies
lying cold
after your privileged soul
felt triggered enough
to trigger fire
into a body that was innocent.
bet you'll never understand
how the positioning of your hands
stands in between life or death
for you.

Number Two: Hear

what does it sound like?
hearing a native language
and calling it a threat.
yelling at minorities
to go back home
to places they never even met
like we didn't forget
you never discovered
this country to begin with,
but I guess the sound of
white privilege is just as
loud as your ignorance

Number Three: Smell

what kind of stench is it?
did you taint the air
with pollution from your
plastic oppression?
fake yet still choking
lives that drown in it,
or is it the smell of smoke?
from burning down
anything that goes against
this nation's founding principles,
but your actions will never
earn you the name "criminal".
you see, I know a word that's
six letters and two syllables.
it cuts deep into every
privileged white person
who thinks they're invincible.

so, maybe you're a racist

for believing that your skin
is superior to all the others.
carrying the weight of white privilege
over your shoulder
while your hate
still lingers around
like bad odors.

Number Four: Taste

what does it taste like?
after feeding on
acts of discrimination
that's done against everyone.
using your silver spoon
to chew on injustice
but spit out the truth
that we're forced to accept.

we always fall victim to neglect
with our actions and intentions
being misconstrued,
if white privilege had a taste
I'd call it a bitter excuse.

Number Five: Sight

how does it look
when you're viewing through
the lens of white privilege?
I bet looks like
a chance at good health
and generational wealth.
looks like climbing to the top
of a mountain on the back
of someone else,
just to get to the top
and claim you had no help.
I bet it looks like
a job that's guaranteed
even if you caught a charge
for selling weed.
it looks like paid leaves.
looks like white women
on movie screens
given the lead role
for Egyptian queens.
it looks like crack vs cocaine,
targeting men of color
and justifying your actions
with the blame on neighborhood gangs.
I bet it looks like getting pulled over
and given a warning,
looks like being aggressive with police
and still given a warning.
looks like not being presumed you're
dangerous or armed and

not losing your life
amid innocent jogging
cause your skin fits the description
of someone guilty of robbing.

it looks like
a family photo
instead of a mugshot.

looks like believing a problem
doesn't exist because it's not
affecting you on the spot.

and sometimes, it looks like me.

you're rocking cornrows and fake procedures.
paying money for the same features
that labeled us monkeys
labeled us creatures,
but the media
giving you all the praise and attention.
cause to be us but not us is always trending
while my Black girls and women
still facing suspensions
in settings where the inventors
can't even flaunt their invention.

oh, but because you're privileged
it's not ghetto
it's art.

well in that case
I bet the artwork looks like
a blank canvas
because every good creation
this nation has ever had
was whited out.

Dear Hip Hop,

I rode the wave
even after they said
it would swallow me whole
and that I may come out vicious,
vulgar and violent.

they were wrong.

I found more answers
in your ocean
than I ever imagined.
found rhythm in the ripples
of your waters
found beauty in the beat
of your current
found love in the lyrics
written in the sand
found my origin
in the depths of your ocean,

nothing surprising there.

just promise me that
you won't allow
great white sharks to take over
and make over your art.
assure me that your shores
will always be a gateway
to a safe space
for us to float freely

promise me that
although your waters
may alter,
your treasures
will never drift away.

Drowning

at the table,
you listen
as if we speak underwater
when we state facts
and give suggestions.
so, our tongues learn
to use your roots
instead of our own.
yet we still drown.

in the bedrooms,
you listen
as if we speak underwater
when we say no
and stop.
so, our breath
loses strength
in a fight for our dignity,
and we still drown.

in the hospitals,
you listen
as if we speak underwater
when we scream in pain
and agony.
so, we lose our lives
producing another.
floating lifelessly
in a blue sea
of red stripes and white stars.

hoping to be seen
to be noticed
to be saved
finally, by someone
other than our self.

Reflections

for years, America has done nothing,
but try to remove the face in the mirror.
desperately attempting to replace it
with the image of its victims.
guilt has crept into its conscious
and strangled its airways
so much that it only breathes
of fear,

fear of revenge.

terror has sketched false photos
of monsters on our skin
only portraying America's
identity within,
wanting reason to label us
as sin or a curse
as evil or dirt
as if malicious acts did not arise
from its flag's "pure" fabric first.

but it did.

white hands steered the boat
white fingers tied the rope
white bodies bombed our hope
white thugs invented this dope
white egos altered our vote
white racists murdered Black folk

yet we're the threat?

America continues to leave
its history's reflection veiled and unaddressed,
but I've learned that hiding
is what cowards tend to do best.

Hey, Black Man

give me a love
that never runs away
cause I have nothing
aimed at you but open arms.
I promise
the only hashtag club
you'll become a member of
is *Man Crush Everyday*
cause this love be daily.

it be fresh and loud
we be hip hop; full of flavor and fire
never turning our volume down
cause I promise
there are no police around,
you can be free around me.
let your wings soar
no need to keep them tucked anymore.
I promise
no one is following you.
you're not stealing anything,
but my heart.

so, give me yours.
melt more, it's okay.
I promise
I won't mock you
for softening
for being vulnerable
for wanting to receive a love
the world refuses to give you.

hey, Black man
it's safe here,
I promise.

Speak with Yo' Heart

As It Was Written

I can imagine
that loving someone
is like writing a poem.
most days it just flows
and comes so naturally.
reminds you
of being true
and how deep you can be,
yet it still requires effort.
still needs you to be thoughtful
and not afraid of error
cause
everything won't perfect.

some days
you'll feel uncertain
because the words that once rhymed
and made sense
are now undefined
and filled with discontent,
it's too intense.
and the problem with this
is that sometimes the writer
views it as a sign to dismiss
their work.
they abandon their craft
because the lack of desired perfection
tears their ego in half.
not understanding most beautiful poems
stem from rough drafts,
that's love.
and in the mist of this confusion,
it's easy to think that comparing
your work to others
may come with some solution.
losing sight

on what's right
in front of you.
unaware of what the next writer
may have gone through.
never seeing crossed out words
the ripped-up pages
with ideas deterred,
love is complicated to observe
especially when you're looking from
someone else's view.
it gets clouded with judgement
and easy to misconstrue,

losing truth.

I just hope that the next time
your lover doesn't decide to rhyme
and go with your flow,
that you'll still hold the pen
and write what you know
cause love….
love is like writing a poem.

Butterflies

they're beautiful when they float
effortlessly through the wind.
they're unique with God's art
painted on their flapping canvases.
they're amazing when they transform,
when they adorn
the skies.

but
they feel funny
when they tickle me, internally.
should I laugh?
maybe I'll just smile
because I like you.

Sappy Book Blues

dear book,
I really like your cover.
are you as appealing
on the inside
as you are on the outside?
now I'm attracted,
now I want to know more.

dear book,
can I place you in my hands?
and run my fingers
through every page
while I take notes of every
story?

dear book,
I like what I'm reading.
your words make me smile
your descriptions are cheerful
your stories bring laughter.

dear book,
I could probably write more.
I could probably be more in-depth,
but I'll just keep it simple
and continue reading.

Falling

leaves remain still,
attached to a branch
until the season is right
until it's the perfect time
for them to fall.
I'm sure they wish
they'd stay connected
to those loving limbs,
free from abandonment
free from stomping grounds.

my love,
please don't treat my heart
like a leaf.

Homes

I would love for this poem
to rhyme and make sense
but sometimes it doesn't,
and that's okay for art
for feelings.

the beauty is that
it always flows.
always knows the direction
it's wanting to go.

it leads without logic
without judgement
without fear.

so, hold me near
because you feel like
home.
I know it sounds crazy,
but when you walk into a space
you know you're destined
to live in,

you don't ask questions.

Dramatic

when you date a poet,
understand that your attitude
will become similes
your emotions
will become metaphors
your actions
will be the starting line
for each stanza.

because yes,
your fingers became
razor blades
as they longed for mine,
making paper machete
out of my skin
using them to decorate
the very room
you decided to sink in
when

you didn't text me back.

Convenient

when our bodies depart,
arms cannot easily hold
fingers cannot easily intertwine.

although
mouths can easily communicate,
they don't.

in that moment,
you realize
maybe it wasn't
real love

just convenience.

Learning Love

I remember when
I wrote a poem about love
without knowing its depths.

I wrote like an outsider
only observing
what my eyes could see
not realizing my heart
could provide
clearer pictures.

I remember how easily
the words flowed
as if they knew me.
how easily
they rolled off my tongue.

now they choke me,
cause love…
love is harder to swallow
than I thought.

Fragile Love

I wrapped his gift
with bubble wrap
and extra paper, extra care.

I placed it inside
a sturdy box.

I warned him
with notes written
for caution.

careful, this heart breaks easily.

Dry Hearts

my heart nurtured flowers
with no water to show for.
attempting to grow gardens
when light was starving
and the soil hardened
around me.

Non-essential

your love is amazing.
showing me paintings
on hidden canvases

making my eyeballs
dance as if
no one is watching

holding me
the way lungs
do air
underwater,

yet you're not
air or water.
so never think,

I need you.

Ending This

I didn't pick up those scissors
on my own.

nope

intuition led me there.
reality placed them
in my sight.
worth positioned them
in my hands.
peace lifted my arm.
God held the rope,

and I cut the ties.

Broken Records

when my body thought
it knew love,
it sang songs
with unfit melodies
fast forwarding to verses
with lyrics still unwritten
forgetting
to be in tune with itself.

Saving Grace

one of the best feelings
you will ever experience
is the feeling you have
after you leave a toxic relationship.
the feeling of happiness
peace
and joy
after being with someone
who's number one priority
was to destroy.

for me,
that someone was anxiety.

the only relationship
that has lasted so long,
four years strong
to be exact.

the person that made me
wear masks in public
always going the extra mile
to make sure my masks
were filled with bright smiles.
not because he was jealous
of letting others see
my inner beauty,
but he wanted to hide
the fact that I was always
so gloomy.

with him,
I became skilled
at hiding my emotions.
laughing at everything
to avoid the fact

that I was internally broken.

laughter is the best medicine, right?

until you find yourself
up at night,
and anxiety cuddles up to you
with arms of pessimistic
delight.
so, you start to think the worst
about everything.

with him,
there was no such thing
as an open relationship.
no room to see other people,
but I tried
escaping anxiety
who had become too much
to handle.
I eventually grew tired
of signing guys up
for love triangles.

and just like any other
toxic relationship,
it was filled with lies.
not to each other,
mainly towards others.

it would usually be in response
to questions like…
"How was your day?" or
"Are you alright?"
I would always lie
and say that I was fine
because explaining to someone
that you have anxiety

is like saying,
"I can see, but I'm blind."

during the later part
of our relationship,
things began to change
for the worst.
he had turned into this person
I didn't recognize
turned me into a person
I didn't recognize.
no longer feeling anxious
worried
and pessimistic.
this time I felt sad
lonely
and nonexistent.
turns out,
he had changed into this person
called depression.

with him,
I wanted to be isolated
so, I shoved
away the people
who surrounded me
with love.
with him,
I cried more.
it became my only escape,
streaming down a river
of my own tears
as depression would begin
to whisper in my ears
and say,
"The only way to get rid
of this suffering pain
is to leave this world,

you'll be happy again."

sadly, his words were so
convincing.
making me think happiness
would be achieved
if I was nonexistent,
and just when I was
about to stop the life
that I was living…
I was grabbed by this person
in a way that was so chilling.

He told me,
"you have so much more
worth fighting for.
your faith is being tested
let me enter the door

to your heart."

so, I did
with no questions asked.
He assured me,
"This battle is not yours
it's mine
sit back and relax."
ever since I let the Lord
take control of my life,
I have a new sense of identity
where there are no masks
in sight.
every smile I wear
is genuine, not fake
because I know now
I can be bended,
but I won't break.

with Him,
I'm grateful for the self-love
I have found.
now I'm in a relationship
that I'm proud
to be in.

for those that are reading,
you're in situation
and the fight feels never-ending
where you just can't seem
to win.
understand, my suffering
only went out
once I let Him in.

Abundant

on this journey,
my heart has been
both the rain and the desert
learning how to weather seasons
of giving and receiving.

learning balance
learning patience
learning that my heart
is elastic, not glass
still careful not to overextend.

realizing
that love may come
from around and within
but its depths lie inside the One
who gifted me
with this pen.